Catholic Update
guide to

Communion

MARY CAROL KENDZIA
Series Editor

ST. ANTHONY MESSENGER PRESS
Cincinnati, Ohio

RESCRIPT

In accord with the *Code of Canon Law*, I hereby grant the Imprimatur
("Permission to Publish") to
Catholic Update Guide to Communion

Most Reverend Joseph R. Binzer
Vicar General and Auxiliary Bishop
Archdiocese of Cincinnati
Cincinnati, Ohio
November 14, 2011

Cover and book design by Mark Sullivan.
Cover image © istockphoto | © Magdalena Kucova

LIBRARY OF CONGRESS CATALOGING-IN-PUBLICATION DATA
Catholic update guide to communion / Mary Carol Kendzia, series editor.
p. cm.
Includes bibliographical references (p.   ).
ISBN 978-1-61636-240-9 (alk. paper)
1. Lord's Supper—Catholic Church. 2. Catholic Church—Doctrines. I. Kendzia,
Mary Carol.
BX2215.3.C44 2012
234'.163—dc23

2011042890

ISBN 978-1-61636-240-9

Published by St. Anthony Messenger Press
28 W. Liberty St.
Cincinnati, OH 45202
www.AmericanCatholic.org
www.SAMPBooks.org

Printed in the United States of America.
Printed on acid-free paper.
12 13 14 15 16   5 4 3 2 1

Contents

About This Series

The Catholic Update guides take the best material from our best-selling newsletters and videos to bring you up-to-the-minute resources for your faith. Topically arranged for these books, the words you'll find in these pages are the same clear, concise, authoritative information you've come to expect from the nation's most trusted faith formation series. Plus, we've designed this series with a practical focus—giving the "what," "why," and "how to" for the people in the pews.

The series takes the topics most relevant to parish life—for example, the Mass, sacraments, Scripture, the liturgical year—and draws them out in a fresh and straightforward way. The books can be read by individuals or used in a study group. They are an invaluable resource for sacramental preparation, RCIA participants, faith formation, and liturgical ministry training, and are a great tool for everyday Catholics who want to brush up on the basics.

The content for the series comes from noted authors such as Thomas Richstatter, O.F.M., Lawrence Mick, Leonard Foley, O.F.M., Carol Luebering, William H. Shannon, and others. Their theology and approach is grounded in Catholic practice and tradition, while mindful of current Church practice and teaching. We blend each author's style and approach into a voice that is clear, unified, and eminently readable.

Enrich your knowledge and practice of the Catholic faith with the helpful topics in the Catholic Update Guide series.

Mary Carol Kendzia
Series Editor

Introduction

The eucharistic sacrifice is the "source and summit of all Christian life." This statement comes from the idea stated in *Lumen Gentium* (11) and may be the teaching that is most often quoted from all the documents of the Second Vatican Council. The bishops reiterated this insight in their document on the life of priests: "For the most Holy Eucharist holds within itself the whole spiritual treasure of the church...the Eucharist is seen as the source and summit of all evangelization" (*Presbyterorum Ordinis*, 5).

As the sacrament of Christ's Body and Blood, the Eucharist is the real presence of Jesus Christ. It is the memorial of Christ's passion and resurrection. It is the breaking of the bread from the Last Supper. It is the holy sacrifice. It is the holy and divine liturgy. It is Holy Communion. It is the Mass. It is the sacrament of sacraments.

While the *Catholic Update Guide to the Mass* focused on the Eucharist as liturgy, the *Catholic Update Guide to Communion* is devoted to the Eucharist as sacrament. With the help of several Catholic Update contributors, we will review this "source and summit" of our Christian lives.

CHAPTER ONE

What Is Communion?

The earliest account of the institution of the Eucharist comes in the First Letter to the Corinthians. St. Paul explained that at supper on the night before Jesus died, the Lord took bread and said, "This is my body that is for you. Do this in remembrance of me." And at the end of the meal Jesus took a cup and said, "This cup is the new covenant in my blood. Do this, as often as you drink it, in remembrance of me" (11:24–25). The Synoptic Gospels tell the same story (see Mark 14:22–24; Matthew 26:26–28; and Luke 22:14–20).

The major elements of the Eucharist, then, are the bread and wine (Jesus calls them his body and blood), the eating and drinking, and his desire that his actions are to serve as a memorial. It is clear that the post-resurrection community of believers took Jesus' legacy seriously and was soon sharing what it called "the Lord's supper."

First, Alfred McBride, O.PRAEM., and John Feister will put the sacrament in its historical context and help us understand the "what" of this sacred gift.

From Meal to Worship

Early Christians understood the Last Supper as a sort of Passover meal. It was held in an "upper room," a place often used for rabbinic Scripture discussions. Upon entering the room, the apostles would have seen a short-legged table surrounded by cushions where they would sit.

On the table was a bowl of saltwater, in memory of the tears shed during the time of slavery in Egypt. A dish of bitter salad recalled their crushing slave days. A container of mashed apples, raisins, and plums coated with cinnamon looked like the bricks they made. Platters of unleavened bread stood next to the large Cup of Blessing filled with wine. A roasted lamb (part of a lamb sacrificed at the temple) symbolized the sacrificial quality of the meal and recalled the blood of a lamb on their doorposts that saved them from the avenging angel in Egyptian times.

Jesus opened the meal with a psalm that praised God for his mighty deeds of salvation during the Exodus. Then he took the bread, gave thanks for it and, breaking tradition, followed this with new words: "Take and eat. This is my body that will be given up for you." This bread was now his body. It would be given up, that is, offered on the cross.

At the end of the meal, Jesus took the Cup of Blessing filled with wine, and instead of making the usual toast he again broke tradition and said, "Take and drink…. This is my blood…. It will be shed for you and for many for the forgiveness of sins." Once more Christ referred to his forthcoming passion where he would shed his blood.

As they drank of the one cup and ate of the one bread, the apostles experienced their unity in Christ. Finally, Christ gave them and their successors the power to celebrate Eucharist: "Do this in remembrance of me." They all sang a psalm and Jesus went forth to his saving death and resurrection.

Gradually the apostles and their successors developed the eucharistic celebration into the structure that endures to this day. They first named it the "Breaking of the Bread," but soon they saw the need to separate the rite from a meal, both because of abuses at meals (1 Corinthians 11:17–22) and because they wanted a more prayerful setting for this act of worship.

This development was reported by a late first-century document, the *Didache* or *Teaching of the Apostles*. The celebration of Eucharist was moved to Sunday in memory of Christ's resurrection. In place of the meal the early Christians created a Liturgy of the Word, somewhat modeled after synagogue prayer, that included readings from Scripture, the singing of psalms, and an instruction.

Around the words of institution they added prayers of thanksgiving, praise, and intercession. By the year AD 150, St. Justin Martyr tells us that the basic structure of the Mass was already in place. These Eucharists were held in people's homes until the year AD 313. On Sundays there were two readings by a lector, a homily by the priest, and then the Eucharistic Prayer followed by the distribution of Communion. And yes, there was a collection —for widows, orphans, and others in need! It is clear that the basic form of the Eucharist took shape very early and has remained remarkably durable for two thousand years.

The Growing Body of Christ

The year 313 was a turning point for Christianity. The persecution of Christians suddenly ended. Constantine gave freedom to Christians and spent great sums of money building basilicas for eucharistic worship. Modest house churches gradually ceased to exist, and stately ceremonies more suited to a huge church environment emerged. Processions, courtly movement in the sanctuary, metered chant (composed by St. Ambrose) and sung litanies that galvanized the voices of thousands, incense and bells, kissing sacred objects, and genuflection became a pattern to accompany the ancient structure of the Eucharist.

The celebrants wore clothes worthy of a Roman senator. Their robes eventually came to be called *vestments*, since they were retained long after fashions changed. The simple plates and cups of house worship became elaborate chalices and patens. This was an inevitable evolution due to social acceptance, organizing an empire-size Church, and ecclesial prosperity.

This era of Christianity witnessed the rise of extraordinary bishops, known now as church fathers, such as Augustine and Chrysostom, whose homilies were rich in theology and pastoral in application. Their genius was to work out theological development in the context of the light generated by the Eucharist and to be attentive to the prayerful hunger and faith of the people. Their theme was "The Body of Christ (Eucharist) builds the Body of Christ (Church)."

The widespread appearance of stunning Gothic cathedrals in medieval Europe signaled an ascendancy of faith. Additionally, the vibrant religious processions for feasts of saints, the enthusiasm for pilgrimages to holy shrines, and the birth of new religious orders led some historians to call these centuries the "Age of Faith."

But alongside these events were troublesome declines in active participation in the Mass. The removal of the assembly from participation in the Eucharist was dramatized by screens of stone or iron that hid the choir and the altar from public view. Monks and priests conducted their corporate liturgy away from the assembly.

The Mass remained in Latin, even though people used their local languages for most other things in their lives. And when the people complained of the growing remoteness of the Mass, they were given Masses said at side altars where the priest faced the wall and prayed in Latin.

The people compensated for their estrangement by asking the priest to hold up the host for them to view and adore: "Hold it higher, sir priest!" Meanwhile, Berengar of Tours heretically taught that Jesus was not really present in the host and that it was only a symbol of his presence. The Church repudiated his views at the Fourth Lateran Council in 1215 by affirming Christ's real presence in the Eucharist and introducing the concept of transubstantiation (the substance of bread becomes the substance, or "being," of Christ) to support this doctrine.

Because many Catholics had ceased receiving Communion, the Council also mandated going to Communion at least once a year, at Easter time. Adoration of the Blessed Sacrament became popular along with other forms of public piety.

Following the posting of Martin Luther's *Ninety-Five Theses* in 1517, it took the Church twenty-eight years to gather its energies and open the Council of Trent to deal with the Reformation. The council fathers called for a renewal of the liturgy.

In 1570, Pope Pius V responded to this call by promoting what would be a standard book for the celebration of Mass for the Western Church. Everything in his decree pertained to the priest celebrant and his action at the altar, including the Liturgy of the Word. The participation of the people would be devotional rather than liturgical. The Mass text was in Latin. (This sturdy Tridentine Mass, named for Trent, was the norm until Vatican II, and is still celebrated today as the "extraordinary form" of Mass in the Roman rite.)

The Jesuits introduced Baroque architecture to churches, in which the choir stalls, screens, and walls were removed. The distance between altar and assembly was shortened so that only an altar railing separated them. The altar was placed against the wall, which was lavishly decorated from floor to ceiling. The tabernacle rested on the altar and above it was a niche provided for exposition and adoration of the Blessed Sacrament.

Sadly, most Masses were "low Masses," generally without music, which the assembly attended in silence. Catholics turned to new schools of spirituality to satisfy their spiritual longings, especially to the Spiritual Exercises of St. Ignatius, to the Carmelite schools, and to the writings of St. Francis de Sales. Eventually, it became clear that a return to the source of the liturgy was needed.

Mass in the Era of Vatican II

The first document approved by the Fathers of the Second Vatican Council (1962–1965) was the Constitution on the Sacred Liturgy (*Sacrosanctum Concilium*) in 1963, but the stirrings of liturgical change had occurred many decades earlier. Benedictines had begun to revive earlier liturgical practices, such as Gregorian chant (from the sixth century), and were studying the roots of Christian liturgy and the ways all Christians once had partici- pated in the Mass. Pope Pius X (1903–1914) encouraged the use of Gregorian chant, frequent reception of Communion, and low- ering the age requirement for First Communion to seven years.

Pope Pius XII's encyclical *Mediator Dei* (1947) lent powerful impetus to the liturgical movement. In 1951 Joseph Jungmann, S.J., published *The Mass of the Roman Rite*, which revealed the complex history of the Mass. In the United States, St. John's Abbey in Collegeville, Minnesota, supported the cause for litur- gical change through its magazine *Orate Fratres*, meaning, "Let us pray, brethren." (This magazine, still in publication today, is now called *Worship*.) Their roster of writers included many of the movers and shakers who rallied the Church in America to the cause of liturgical renewal.

And so by the time Vatican II assembled, the groundwork was firmly laid by patient scholarship, hundreds of meetings, and countless articles. With relatively little debate and very small opposition, the Constitution on the Sacred Liturgy was approved by the Council Fathers—2,147 in favor to 4 opposed. The sonorous words of that document reached a high point when it declared, "The liturgy is the summit toward which the activity of the Church is directed; at it the same time it is the font from which all her power flows" (10).

In the last part of the twentieth century the application of the document began and a number of changes were introduced. The priest now faced the people. Vernacular languages replaced the Latin. People shook hands at the greeting of peace. The congregation was asked to participate actively in the Mass, to sing and pray at various times. People were invited to receive Communion either in the hand or on the tongue and to stand at its reception. They were offered the chalice so they could communicate under both species, the eucharistic bread and wine.

Both laity and religious could distribute Communion as extraordinary ministers. Married deacons appeared, to assist the priest at Mass and to preach homilies. Entrance processions were added. People brought up the gifts at the presentation of the offerings. Priests abandoned what some called "fiddleback" chasubles for robelike replacements. Mass readings provided a three-year series of Scripture in which large sections of the Bible would be heard. Homilies, which had become lectures or announcements on just about any topic, were expected to explain Scripture and help the assembly apply it to everyday life. Church architecture became functional and minimalist in decoration—a sign of the times. Instead of the long "shoe box" church building, a wider auditorium model appeared. Guitar Masses surfaced and new hymns were composed and led to many arguments about taste and suitability.

None of these changes happened without some degree of anger and discomfort. Indeed, some experimentation went over the top. But in fact the amazing thing is how little disturbance actually occurred. The dreams of the liturgical movement were fulfilled and expanded. People saw that they could enrich their spirituality by focusing on the celebration of the Eucharist.

One conclusion we can draw from this sketch of the history of the Mass is that changes, whether large or small, have been occurring since the Last Supper but the basics have never changed. In this sense the celebration of the Eucharist is a reality both stable and dynamic. The noble core of the Eucharist, which began in the Upper Room and migrated to urban cathedral and village church alike, has withstood the tumults of history—and always will. And for this dynamic stability, we praise and thank God!

The Real Presence

What we have in this sacrament are not simply bread and wine that symbolize Jesus Christ. Rather, we have under the appearances of bread and wine his unique, true presence. It was this faith conviction about the real presence of Jesus in the Eucharist that led Elizabeth Seton to become a Catholic. When she first learned what Catholics believe she wrote to her sister, "How happy would we be if we believed what these dear souls believe, that they possess God in the Sacrament and that he remains in their churches and is carried to them when they are sick."

Ask Catholics about the real presence of Jesus in the Eucharist and you're likely to hear a variety of personal experiences. John Feister writes of a man he knew from a faith-sharing group who was considered a pillar of the parish. He was always available for parish committees, helped with the parish festival, occasionally led the rosary during prayer services, and was very devoted to his family.

On one occasion, the man conveyed to the faith-sharing group an experience of the real presence of Christ that had occurred in a quiet moment of prayer one Sunday after he had gone to Communion. On that Sunday, he had visualized the body and blood of Jesus, consumed in the form of bread and wine, breaking down into smaller and smaller pieces, all the way down to the tiniest element, being carried to every part of his own body by his beating heart. He felt literally "nourished by Jesus" throughout his whole being.

The man relayed that he also felt deeply connected to those around him. He felt the Eucharist, the presence of Jesus, at the very center of his being, and at that point, he felt connected to that same central point in everyone else who had just received Communion. He experienced, in a mysterious way, the real presence of Jesus, an experience of both transcendence with God and of communion with the Body of Christ, the Church—indeed, with the whole world. This man's experience points to an authentically Catholic understanding of the Eucharist.

Recent years have seen a growing concern about Catholics' understanding of the real presence of Jesus in the Eucharist. Some surveys show that a number of practicing Catholics are not clear about the doctrine of real presence. Some think of consecrated bread and wine as only symbols of Jesus' presence rather than a genuine change of bread and wine into the Body and Blood of Christ, which is the long-standing Catholic understanding.

In 1999 a group of U.S. bishops petitioned their fellow bishops to join them in addressing the problem. They described this confusion about the real presence as a "grave" situation. The first result of the bishops' efforts was the 2001 pastoral statement *The Real Presence of Jesus Christ in the Sacrament of the Eucharist: Basic Questions and Answers*, published by the U.S. Conference of Catholic Bishops. That document was introduced to the bishops' conference as a resource for pastors and religious educators.

Why does Communion still look like bread and wine?

This question may point to the greatest stumbling block for belief in the real presence, and we are not the first generation of Christians to ask the question. Yet each generation has found the answer through the eyes of faith. The Church teaches that the transformation of bread and wine into the Body and Blood of Christ is taking place "below the surface"—that is, in the "substance" of the bread and wine. What can be seen, tasted, touched, and smelled is indeed the same as the bread and wine, but there has been a real change that we require faith to accept.

In brief, we Catholics believe that, at their deepest reality but not in physical characteristics, the bread and wine become the Body and Blood of Christ when they are consecrated at Eucharist. After consecration, they are no longer bread and wine: They are the Body and Blood of Jesus. As St. Thomas Aquinas observed, Christ is not quoted as saying, "*This bread* is my body," but "*This* is my body" (*Summa Theologiae*, III, q. 78, a. 5).

Once the bread and wine become the Body and Blood of Christ, they remain so as long as the "appearances of bread and wine remain" (see also *CCC,* #1377). They never revert back to bread and wine because a real and permanent change has taken place. That is why we reserve the Blessed Sacrament in a tabernacle in our churches.

Christ is fully present in every fragment of the consecrated Host and fully present in every drop of consecrated Blood. So a person receiving only the consecrated bread or wine receives Christ fully. Yet it is preferable, a more complete sign of the heavenly banquet, to receive the sacrament under both forms rather than under only one.

If the consecrated bread and wine are Christ's real presence, why are they still considered symbols?

It is particularly fitting that Christ should come to us in the

Eucharist, the bishops explain in *The Real Presence of Jesus Christ in the Sacrament of the Eucharist*, for

> Jesus Christ gives himself to us in a form that employs the symbolism inherent in eating bread and drinking wine. Furthermore, being present under the appearances of bread and wine, Christ gives himself to us in a form that is appropriate for human eating and drinking. Also, this kind of presence corresponds to the virtue of faith, for the presence of the Body and Blood of Christ cannot be detected or discerned by any way other than faith.

The bishops here are reminding us that, even though real—and not merely symbolic—change has taken place, there is still tremendous symbolism at work. All sacraments use symbols, because symbols help us understand the deepest connections between things. Here are two examples. Just as food nourishes us, God nourishes us. Or again, just as a grain of wheat must die to become bread, so too must we.

The symbolism of the Eucharist is a deep and nearly inexhaustible topic. It in no way diminishes the fact that a real, substantial change has taken place. In the bishops' words, "God uses...the symbolism inherent in the eating of bread and the drinking of wine at the natural level to illuminate the meaning of what is being accomplished in the Eucharist through Jesus Christ."

Why is the Eucharist reserved in the tabernacle?

Although the sacrament could be consumed in its entirety at Mass, the Church, from early times, has reserved the consecrated bread that was not consumed so the Eucharist might be taken to the dying as "food for the journey" (*viaticum*). It is also used for the sick of the community and for those who were, for some good reason, unable to be present for the community celebration.

Another pastoral practice arose as, centuries ago, the faithful began to see the value of being in the presence of the sacramental Body and Blood. Exposition of the Blessed Sacrament allows an opportunity to adore God, whether in eucharistic exposition or benediction or in eucharistic processions. The Body of Christ in the form of bread in the tabernacle provides an excellent opportunity for private prayer. "Many holy people well known to American Catholics, such as St. John Neumann, St. Elizabeth Ann Seton, St. Katharine Drexel, and St. Damien of Molokai, practiced great personal devotion to Christ present in the Blessed Sacrament," the bishops wrote.

The presence of the Blessed Sacrament is cause for the greatest reverence, the bishops insist, both during and after the celebration of the Eucharist. Canon law states that the tabernacle in church is to be in a place "distinguished, conspicuous, beautifully decorated, and suitable for prayer."

Further, "According to the tradition of the Latin Church, one should genuflect in the presence of the tabernacle containing the reserved sacrament," the bishops remind us. Fasting before receiving Communion, in accordance with Church law, is another form of reverence for the sacrament.

What if someone who doesn't believe in the real presence receives Communion?

Even though the Body and Blood of Christ are really present in the Eucharist, faith plays a strong role in how we respond to (or accept) that presence. It is commonly asked whether or not a nonbeliever has received the Body and Blood of Christ if he or she receives Communion. The answer is yes, in the sense that what the nonbeliever has consumed is really Christ. But a lack of belief prevents someone from receiving the spiritual benefit of the Eucharist, "communion with Christ."

Questions sometimes arise about a person receiving Communion while in a state of mortal sin. Once again, the disposition of the recipient cannot change the fact that Jesus is truly present in the elements of the Eucharist. "The question here is thus not primarily about the nature of the Real Presence, but about how sin affects the relationship between an individual and the Lord," write the bishops. "Before one steps forward to receive the Body and Blood of Christ in Holy Communion, one needs to be in a right relationship with the Lord and his Mystical Body, the Church—that is, in a state of grace, free of all mortal sin. While sin damages, and can even destroy, that relationship, the sacrament of Penance can restore it."

How else is Jesus really present to us?

The Church teaches that Christ is present to us in other ways at the Eucharist besides in the Blessed Sacrament. He is present in the priest, the assembly gathered to worship, and in the holy Scriptures.

It is indeed a mystery that God became flesh in Jesus and that Jesus becomes present to us in sacrament and Scripture. Mystery, the bishops say, refers not to a puzzling reality but rather to

> aspects of God's plan of salvation for humanity, which has already begun but will be completed only with the end of time.
>
> St. Paul explained that the mysteries of God may challenge our human understanding or may even seem to be foolishness, but their meaning is revealed to the People of God through Jesus Christ and the Holy Spirit (see 1 Corinthians 1:18–25; 2:6–10; Romans 16:25–27; Revelation 10:7). The Eucharist is a mystery because it participates in the mystery of Jesus Christ and God's plan to save humanity through Christ.

Questions for Reflection

1. When you next go to Mass, consider how many of the same elements of what we celebrate today were instituted in the early Church. What does this connection to the past mean to you?

2. How do you see the consecrated Body of Christ: as food to be eaten or an object to be adored?

3. What is important to you about receiving the Body and Blood of Christ in Communion?

CHAPTER TWO

Why Did Jesus Give Us This Extraordinary Gift?

Why did the Creator make the world? Why did the Holy One get involved in human history? Why did the Father send his Son to be the savior of humankind? The answer to these and many other mysteries is simple: God is love. And that is the answer to the question about why Jesus gave us the Eucharist. It was his love for humankind that prompted him to say, "As the Father has loved me, so I have loved you. Abide in my love" (John 15:9). The Eucharist is an expression of God's love for mankind, a sign of the union Jesus wants with his disciples.

Jesus prayed "that they all may be one. As you, Father, are in me and I in you, may they also may be in us.... I made your name known to them, and I will make it known, so that the love with which you have loved me may be in them, and I in them" (John 17:20, 26). The Eucharist *is* a sacrament of unity.

This chapter will explore how Communion unites us as a community and unites us with Christ himself.

The Unitive Power of Eucharist

Liturgist Fr. Lawrence E. Mick sees the unitive power of the Eucharist in its relationship to the Jewish Passover meal, noting that the early Christians saw the Eucharist as the fulfillment of the Passover. The Synoptic Gospels cast the Lord's Supper as the Passover meal; John, however, saw Jesus as the Paschal Lamb sacrificed on the cross. St. Paul also links Christ's death and resurrection with the Passover in Corinthians: "Clean out the old yeast, so that you may be a new batch, as you really are unleavened. For our paschal lamb, Christ, has been sacrificed. Therefore let us celebrate the festival, not with the old yeast, the yeast of malice and evil, but with the unleavened bread of sincerity and truth" (1 Corinthians 5:7–8).

To understand the Eucharist, then, we must understand the meaning of the Passover celebration. The roots of this festival are very ancient, even preceding the Exodus of the Jews from Egypt. The later Passover is really a combination of two celebrations: a nomadic tribal sacrifice of a lamb whose blood is sprinkled on the tent pegs to ward off evil spirits, and an agrarian ritual marking spring and the harvest of new grain with the use of unleavened bread. As nomads settled among local farmers, these two celebrations were combined.

The Hebrew Scriptures, however, gives a new meaning to these combined rituals by linking them to the events of the Exodus. As part of that event, God sent a series of plagues to afflict the Egyptians. In response to Moses' warning about the death of the firstborn by a destroying angel, the Israelites slaughtered lambs and marked their homes with the blood, thus warding off this evil. Then, in the shadow of that plague, they fled Egypt in haste, with bread unleavened (see Exodus 12:21–36.)

For the Jews, then, the Passover is a celebration of the Exodus. It is a feast of liberation, rejoicing in God's wondrous acts on their behalf that set them free from slavery. The Exodus was also the event that established Israel as a people, as God's chosen people. One might draw a comparison to our Fourth of July rituals here in the United States, which celebrate our independence and our identity as a nation. Passover had—and still has—a similar significance for the Jewish people.

In at least one significant respect, though, the Jewish understanding of Passover is quite different from the way we Americans think of the Fourth of July. We celebrate an event that happened more than two hundred years ago. We celebrate our continuing freedom, but we think of that past event as long gone and out of reach. Even though some of us may dress up in colonial garb, we don't really think of ourselves as being present at the signing of the Declaration of Independence or of taking part in the Revolutionary War that achieved our freedom.

For the Jews, on the other hand, remembering the Exodus is more than just a mental recall. The book of Exodus commands the Jewish father to explain the meaning of the feast this way: "You shall tell your child on that day, 'It is because of what the LORD did for me when I came out of Egypt'" (13:8). All Jews are to celebrate the feast as though they had been alive at the time of the Exodus. They see the feast as somehow bringing them into contact with that ancient event. This is the concept we try to express with the term *memorial* (*anamnesis* in Greek). Through the ritual observance, the contemporary Jew not only remembers the past but also relives it.

At the same time, the memorial celebration of the Passover also proclaims God's continuing liberating action on behalf of God's people in the present day and looks forward to the fulfillment of God's promises for complete salvation when the Messiah comes. Just as God acted in the past, God continues to act in the present and will act in the future to save us.

Christ's Exodus

The Church has long understood that the celebration of the Eucharist brings us into contact with the saving actions of Christ. That is the way we are able to share in his sacrifice, his exodus through death to resurrected life. His sacrifice is not repeated; he died once for all and death has no more power over him. But his sacrifice is also eternal, and our enacting the ritual of the Eucharist enables us to enter into that eternal act.

22

Though the Church has long held the basic view that the Eucharist brings us into contact with Christ's sacrifice, it has not endorsed any theological explanation of how this happens. One way to understand what happens is to recognize that the core of Christ's sacrifice was his commitment to the Father's will, clearly expressed in the agony in the garden: "Not my will but yours be done" (Luke 22:42). This commitment led him to the cross and resurrection at one point in history, but ultimately Christ's will is eternally united with the Father's will.

Christ is forever victim, forever priest. When we celebrate the Eucharist, we are invited to enter into that eternal act, aligning our wills with the Father's will as Jesus did. Thus we become one with Christ and share in his sacrificial act. This can help us to realize the breadth of the commitment we make when we "do this in memory" of Jesus.

What did Jesus mean by "this"? What are we to do in memory of him? Pope Benedict XVI addressed this question in a homily at World Youth Day in Germany in August 2005. "Jesus did not instruct us," Benedict said, "to repeat the Passover meal, which in any event, given that it is an anniversary, is not repeatable at will. He instructed us to enter into his 'hour.'" The pope goes on to suggest that Jesus' hour is the "hour in which love triumphs" and that we share his hour if we "allow ourselves, through the celebration of the Eucharist, to be drawn into that process of transformation that the Lord intends to bring about."

In memory of Jesus, then, we are to be transformed by adopting his attitude of love and his commitment to the Father's will. We share his sacrifice not only by carrying out the ritual of the Mass but also by living our lives in accord with God's will. The Amen that we sing at the end of the Eucharistic Prayer at every Mass commits us to a whole way of life. Our Eucharist is authentic only if it expresses the meaning of our whole lives. What we are to do in memory of Jesus is to live and love as he did.

When Jesus described his ministry in Luke's Gospel, he quoted Isaiah:

> The Spirit of the Lord is upon me,
> He has sent me to proclaim release to the captives
>   and recovery of sight to the blind,
>   to let the oppressed go free. (Luke 4:18–19)

Those words echo the Passover celebration of God as a liberator of the oppressed, and they stand as a challenge to us to embrace Christ's mission as our own.

In the Eucharist our God has shown love in the extreme, over-turning all those criteria of power that too often govern human relations, and radically affirming the criterion of service: "Whoever wants to be first must be last of all and the servant of all" (Mark 9:35). It is not by chance that the Gospel of John contains no account of the institution of the Eucharist but instead relates the washing of feet (see John 13:1–20). By bending down to wash the feet of his disciples, Jesus explains the meaning of the Eucharist unequivocally. In 1 Corinthians 11:17–22, 27–34, St. Paul vigorously reaffirms the impropriety of a eucharistic celebration that lacks charity expressed by practical sharing with the poor.

We cannot delude ourselves: By our mutual love and, in particular, by our concern for those in need, we will be recognized as true followers of Christ (see John 13:35; Matthew 25:31–46). This will be the criterion by which our eucharistic celebrations are judged.

Why Did Jesus Come to Earth?

Scripture scholar Stephen Doyle reflects on the reason why Jesus came to earth, and then ultimately why Jesus gave us the gift of the Eucharist. He challenges the idea that Jesus came because Adam sinned. He raises a most significant issue: Would Jesus have taken on human nature even if the human race had not fallen from grace? Calling on a theology promoted by the Franciscans since the Middle Ages, Fr. Doyle thinks Jesus was from the start destined to "dwell among us." He thinks St. Paul would agree.

As Doyle writes:

> In Paul's mature theology in Ephesians and Colossians, he doesn't give the impression that Jesus Christ, the

God-Man, arrived upon the scene because of Adam. Jesus, not Adam, is the focal point of the plan of God. We do not thank Adam for the coming of Jesus, for the Incarnation already was primary and central to the plan of God. God predestined Jesus from all eternity. That is the absolute primacy and predestination of Christ.

This theological view has been the consistent view of Franciscans since the Middle Ages, championed especially by John Duns Scotus (1266–1308). In Scotus's view, the Word of God became flesh not because Adam and Eve sinned but because from all eternity God wanted Christ to be creation's most perfect work, the model and crown of creation and humanity—the glorious destination toward which all creation is straining. In his view, the divine Word would have been incarnated in Christ even if the first man and woman had never sinned.

Another point made by Scotus and the Franciscans is this: It was not Adam who was the pattern or blueprint that God used in shaping Christ. It was the other way around. In God's mind, the second Person of the Blessed Trinity was the model from which Adam and Eve and the whole human race were created. Many of the fathers, particularly of the Eastern Church, as well as brilliant theologians such as the Spanish Jesuit Francisco Suarez (1548–1617); the bishop of Geneva, St. Francis de Sales (1567–1622); and, closer to our own time, Karl Rahner, s.j., all built their theology and spirituality on a similar way of thinking. Rahner states it succinctly: "God's design for the incarnation of the Logos is an absolute one, and made by him before any human, free decision (like that of Adam and Eve) could have been the motive."

Restoring All Things in Christ

In Paul's Letter to the Ephesians, he speaks about God's "plan for the fullness of time," in which God wants "to gather up all things in him"—that is, in Christ—"things in heaven and things on earth." The phrase, "to gather up all things in him," is a rather free translation of Paul's Greek, which means to bring to a head again, to put something back where it belongs, to restore (see Ephesians 1:7–10).

When we restore a piece of furniture, we put it back in the condition it was in when it left the hands of its maker. We return it to the way he wanted it to be—to the original blueprint, so to speak. Paul intentionally chose this word, knowing that the way God intended things to be—that is, centered in Christ—had gone awry and needed to be restored.

Christ would have come under any conditions but, given the sin of Adam, the way he actually came was as the redeemer of the universe—a universe that was made for himself. Just as the rebellion of Adam and Eve, our first parents, had its repercussions on all of creation, so does the coming of Jesus initiate the process of restoration not only of humanity but of all of creation to himself.

The various and far-flung parts of creation make sense only when they come together in Christ. It helps to look at all created things as if they are scattered pieces of a beautiful picture puzzle. It's only when the pieces are put back in their proper places that they form the original image of Christ, thus displaying their true beauty and meaning.

With a magnificent proclamation of the role of Christ, Paul lets us know just what Jesus is in charge of. He is Lord of all things. Everything! The cosmos! The universe! The past! The future! Every person, place, or thing, real or imagined! Jesus does not fit into their system, he is the system! "In him all things hold together!" (Colossians 1:17).

According to Paul, there never was, is, or will be any reality that was not created for the sake of Jesus Christ. St. Francis de Sales, in his *Treatise on the Love of God*, spells out this vision quite beautifully: "Almighty God, in his eternal plan and design for all that he would create, first of all intended and willed that which he loved the most: our Savior. And then he planned for the creation of other creatures in the proper order for which they were necessary for the service, honor and glory of that beloved Son, Jesus Christ."

In Paul's view of creation, therefore, there is nothing in this world that makes sense apart from Jesus Christ. Every creature in some way points to Christ. Indeed, if the singing of the birds and the humming of the insects could be formed into a chorus, and if the rustling breeze and tinkling rain could have a voice, and the roar of the ocean could be put into words, they would all have one thing to say: "We were made for the sake of Jesus Christ."

Francis of Assisi shared a similar vision. He saw the whole family of creation as profoundly related to Christ. And when the Word of God entered history at the Incarnation and dwelt among us, St. Francis saw this as a cause for celebration among all creatures.

This sense that all creatures are somehow interconnected in Christ is the reason Francis could rhapsodize about "Brother Sun and Sister Moon." His *Canticle of the Creatures*, in which he praised the Creator through Brother Sun and Sister Moon and all the creatures, is not poetic overstatement. It is the practical expression of his theological and spiritual vision. Thus, it is no coincidence that Francis is the patron saint of ecology. He perceived this world as Mother Earth and recognized that it is the home of him whom he loved: Jesus Christ. For Francis, care and concern for creation are care and concern for Jesus' own home.

Eucharist and the Communion of Saints

In the thirteenth century St. Thomas Aquinas was clear in his teaching that the bread and wine truly become the Body and Blood of the Lord, but he saw this transformation as a step on the way to the real purpose of the Eucharist. The true goal of the sacrament, he taught, is the unity of the Church. Another way to put this is to say that Christ did not give us the Eucharist to transform bread and wine into his body and blood. It does that, of course; but further, Christ gave us this sacrament to transform *us* into his Body. That is the goal of the Eucharist and the meaning of Communion. As St. John Chrysostom put it: "What is this bread? The Body of Christ. What becomes of those who participate in this bread? The Body of Christ."

In our own time, Pope John Paul II insisted in his apostolic letter *The Day of the Lord*: "It is also important to be ever mindful that communion with Christ is deeply tied to communion with our brothers and sisters. The Sunday eucharistic gathering is an experience of brotherhood, which the celebration should demonstrate clearly" (44).

The sacramental body exists for the sake of the mystical body. It is interesting that, in the first thousand years of the Church's history, Christians spoke of the Church as the real body of Christ and the sacrament as the mystical body. In the last thousand years, however, we have reversed the terms, calling the sacrament the real presence and the Church the mystical body of Christ. The key is that these two are intimately linked, and the core of the mystery of the Eucharist can be found in this link. The body of Christ shares the Body and Blood of Christ to become more fully the body of Christ.

William Shannon adds another dimension to the unitive and loving power of the Eucharist. He tells this story about a parish priest on a small Greek island in the Aegean Sea. One day a visitor asked the pastor, "How many people usually worship here on Sunday?" The priest's answer was, "Oh, about ten to twelve thousand, I would suppose." The visitor was somewhat bewildered. "This is a tiny island," she said, "and the church is small. Where do all these people come from and how can they possibly fit into so small a church building?"

The priest smiled and then said to the visitor, "All the people who ever lived on this island since it received the gospel message are still here. Just think of what we say in the sacred liturgy: 'Therefore with all the angels and the saints and the whole company of the faithful we praise your glory forever.' Don't you realize," he added, "that when we sing the Trisagion [Holy, Holy, Holy] we are joining with all the holy ones who have ever worshiped in this church?"

How appropriate it is for us to be aware that when we gather to celebrate the Eucharist, many more are present and active than mortal vision is able to see. It is worth noting too that it is not they who join us but we who join them. We and the saints are related as friends, especially friends around the altar, but also friends in carrying on the unfinished tasks that they left to us.

The Eucharist is preeminently the sign and bearer of God's mercy and grace. True, the forgiveness of sins belongs to baptism, and, as it later developed in the Church, to the sacrament that we call penance, or the sacrament of reconciliation. But there is a sense in which it is the Eucharist that is preeminently the sacrament of forgiveness. That's why we pray, at Eucharist, "Lamb of God, you take away the sins of the world."

Karl Rahner, in a small tract on the sacraments called *The Sacraments of the Church*, writes that the Eucharist "simply cannot be put on a level with the other sacraments and listed along with them." That is why he begins his study of the sacraments not in the usual way—with baptism—but with the Eucharist. Fr. Henri de Lubac, another Jesuit theologian who helped shape the post–Vatican II Church, has said that the Eucharist is "sacrament in the highest sense of the word, *sacramentum sacramentorum.*" It embodies the whole mystery of salvation. While the Church exists at all times, it is at the Eucharist, the "source and summit of Catholic worship," that the Church achieves its highest actuality. The Eucharist is, indeed, holy things for holy people.

The term *communio sanctorum*, then, is a window not only into the communion of saints but also into the mystery of the Eucharist. For it means at once a communion of "holy people" as well as a communion of "holy things." Indeed, by extension it could embrace the sacred communion of life that is God's good creation. It unifies.

In its widest sense, the communion of saints is about what Elizabeth Johnson calls, "a communal participation in the gracious holiness of God." When we participate in the Eucharist, we join all the saints in that holy and wondrous communion.

One-sided Love?

If it seems that God is doing all the loving, even when we celebrate the Eucharist as a community, you have discovered the profound truth about grace. We do not earn God's love; it is freely, generously, even prodigally given. This mind-set is one of the chief topics of the preaching and writing of Franciscan friar Richard Rohr over the past several decades. He tells us that the great, central theme of the Bible is grace, God's favor. God's love is literally unaccountable: it can't be put in any ledger of accounts.

Yet the mind-set of merit, of buying, selling, and earning, is common. Until you can give up that mind-set you cannot understand the concept of grace or truly experience it. A biblical image for that is the banquet or meal. That's true in the Old Testament and even more so in the New Testament. Open table fellowship is Jesus' most common audiovisual aid. He gives us the meal as the great image of his unconditional love— a different consciousness, a different way of reading reality.

Pause and consider this carefully: God's love is determined by God's goodness and is no way dependent on us. God tells us, "I am being true to who I am in loving you." If you want to get God, if you want to pray right, say, "OK, God, you've got to do it. Your reputation is at stake. You've got to show me your goodness because I've told the people you're good. You've got to be a Father to me and I will be a son or daughter to you." Thus the love begins. That is the freedom of God's love that Jesus came to proclaim. We experience it in the Eucharist.

Jesus' image for this is the banquet. We hear the parable of the wedding banquet in Matthew 22 and in Luke 14. A king is having a wedding feast for his son and sends out his servants with invitations. Yet many on his list have excuses, even very reasonable excuses. One is getting married, another has a deal on a cow coming in, and so on. (It's not the red-hot sins of passion that keep people from God. More often it's business as usual.) Eventually the king implores his servants to search for anyone who will come—talk them into it, he says! Tell them it's free, tell them that they don't have to have a ticket. Make sure that my house is full.

In Matthew's telling there is a highly symbolic addition, where a guest is thrown out for not wearing a wedding garment. One way to understand that is the wedding garment of a ready heart. We need to have an openness and desire for God's grace. We've got to yearn for it or we will not be ready for it. Before the parable of the wedding feast, in Luke 14:12, Jesus says when you give a lunch or a dinner don't ask your friends, brothers, relations, or rich neighbors, for fear that they might repay you. Then you'd be back into the meritocracy game. They might invite you in return out of courtesy. Jesus is telling his followers: Get out of the worthiness game entirely. When you have a party, invite poor, crippled, lame, blind people so that they cannot pay you back. This will mean you are fortunate.

We see this grace at work in the story of the wedding feast at Cana in John's Gospel, and we see it at the Last Supper. In the Gospels, the banquet is a wonderful symbol of God's free and unconditional love—a love that is often ignored or rejected. It's still hard for us to believe. God is trying to give away God. And no one wants God. We seem to prefer the worthiness system, where we earn what we get. But that's not God's invitation; that's not Eucharist.

Questions for Reflection

1. How do you answer the basic question of this chapter, "Why did Jesus give us the Eucharist?"
2. Does the idea that Jesus would have come to earth even if Adam had not sinned make any difference to you?
3. Why would Jesus share himself with us even though we say, "Lord, I am not worthy"?

CHAPTER THREE

How Do We Receive Communion?

If we are asking how bread and wine become the Body and Blood of Christ, our most honest answer must be, "By the will of God." The God who said "Let it be" in creating the world certainly has the power to change bread and wine into the Body and Blood of Christ. It was that same will of God by which the Word became flesh and pitched his tent among us. If God can become man, then certainly bread and wine can be the vehicle of Christ's real presence.

If we are asking how what looks, tastes, and smells like bread and wine can really be the Body and Blood of Christ, we are talking about a change that the Church, for want of a better term, calls "transubstantiation." This doctrine is our human way of explaining the possibility of such a change.

If we are asking how the Eucharist is celebrated and administered, we must review some of the legal and liturgical aspects of protecting and handing on this most precious gift. Human beings surround whatever they value with law and customs. Canon law and liturgical rubrics support respect for and use of this blessed sacrament of Eucharist.

By the Power of the Holy Spirit

In his 2004 message *Eucharist and Mission*, Pope John Paul II put the matter of how bread and wine can become the Body and Blood of Christ very simply when he said, "The bread and wine, fruit of human hands, is transformed through the power of the Holy Spirit into the Body and Blood of Christ."

At Mass there is a prayer and gesture (hands over the gifts) known as the *epiclesis* (the Greek term means "calling down upon"), in which the priest asks the Father to send the Holy Spirit so that the bread and wine (the offerings) may become the Body and Blood of Christ. This liturgical action occurs just before the words of institution, that is, before the priest repeats the words of Jesus: "This is my body…. This is my blood."

Early in the second century St. Ignatius of Antioch, in his Letter to the Smyrnaeans, described the Eucharist as the Savior's flesh. Later in that century St. Justin Martyr wrote in explanation of the faith that Christians regard the Eucharist not as ordinary food but as the flesh and blood of Christ.

An eighth-century priest and teacher known as St. John of Damascus formulated a synthesis or compilation of Christian doctrine in which he addressed this issue and said, "You ask how the bread becomes the Body of Christ, and the wine...the Blood of Christ. I shall tell you: the Holy Spirit comes upon them and accomplishes what surpasses every word and thought."

Jesus said, "This is my body...this is my blood." He did not explain how the change from bread and wine happened. He simply gave his disciples a memorial, a mystery of faith. The New Testament writers did not so much probe the mystery as promote it.

The belief that a real change took place at the consecration is well attested to in the early Church. St. Irenaeus, for example, who lived in the second century, wrote a masterful compendium of arguments against heresies. In that book he explains that our bodies are nourished by the Body and Blood of the Lord in the Eucharist. He says "the mingled cup and the manufactured bread receive the Word of God," that in the Eucharist (he in fact uses that term) the Body and the Blood of Christ are made.

Since the days of Irenaeus, Church leaders and theologians have discussed the Eucharist and suggested terms that might be used to describe the change from bread and wine into Christ's Body and Blood. St. John Chrysostom called it "transformation." St. Ambrose called it "transfiguration." St. John of Damascus called it "transmutation."

In the ninth century St. Paschasius Radbertus wrote a treatise on the Eucharist, insisting that "the substance of bread and wine is changed into Christ's body and blood." His emphasis on a "substantial" change found support in the eleventh century when a Roman council officially taught that the bread and wine were "substantially changed" into the Body and Blood of Christ.

St. Thomas Aquinas, in his *Summa Theologiae*, addressed the question of whether bread can be converted into the Body of Christ and concluded that "the whole substance of the bread is changed into the whole substance of Christ's body, and the whole substance of the wine into the whole substance of Christ's blood." This substantial conversion, he said, "can be called transubstantiation" (IIIa, 75,4). Several Church councils (Fourth Lateran in 1215, Lyons II in 1274, Florence in 1439, and Trent in the sixteenth century) also used the term.

Transubstantiation is at present the most commonly used descriptive word for the eucharistic change. It is an effort to show that what we believe is not contrary to reason, even if we cannot fully understand it.

Using philosophical categories, theologians make a distinction between a substance and its accidents. A substance is described as "that which a thing is." Accidents are qualities that "inhere" in a substance, such as its color, shape, texture, odor, and the like. Experience and reason show that accidents do not always convey what a substance is. A substance can have the accidents of something else, as when a confectioner makes candy that looks like, smells like, and tastes like bacon. It's not bacon (it's candy) but it has all the accidents of bacon. In a similar way, what looks like, smells like, and tastes like bread could in fact (without defying reason) be Christ's Body.

This explanation does not resolve the mystery of the Eucharist; it is simply an effort to explain it. Although the term *transubstantiation* has a long history in the Church's efforts to express this faith conviction about the change from bread and wine into Christ's body and blood, it is possible that future generations of Catholics may select a different term. After all, the Church is continually trying to explain the unexplainable.

Intercommunion

One of the more sensitive issues regarding the Eucharist is the question of intercommunion, that is, whether non-Catholics can be admitted to Holy Communion or whether Catholics can receive communion in non-Catholic churches. According to Thomas Richstatter, O.F.M., the fundamental meaning of any sacrament can be found in the prayers that accompany the sacramental action. In each of the seven sacraments we invoke the Holy Spirit and petition the Spirit to make us holy and to build up the body of Christ. This petition is the key to understanding the sacrament: The primary petition of the Eucharistic Prayer is for unity in Christ.

We ask that the Spirit change the bread and wine into the Body and Blood of Christ so that we who eat and drink might be changed into the body of Christ. "Make holy, therefore, these gifts, we pray, by sending down your Spirit upon them like the dewfall, so that they may become for us the Body and Blood of our Lord, Jesus Christ.... Humbly we pray that, partaking of the Body and Blood of Christ, we may be gathered into one by the Holy Spirit" (Eucharistic Prayer II). "Grant that we, who are nourished by the Body and Blood of your Son and filled with his Holy Spirit, may become one body, one spirit in Christ" (Eucharistic Prayer III). The other Eucharistic Prayers have similar invocations.

If "unity" is at the heart of Eucharist, why can't all Christians—Protestants, Orthodox, Catholics—share Holy Communion?

Different Christian denominations answer this question in various ways. Some Christians favor "open Communion." This is the position that says no one can stop a baptized person who believes in Jesus Christ from receiving Communion in any Church. They would say that open Communion is the preferred option because the holy supper is a source of unity—a means by which unity among Christians can be achieved. This, however, is not the official Catholic position.

Other Christians believe that the condition for receiving Communion in another church is unity of faith in the real presence. In this perspective, intercommunion will be possible when the Christian Churches reach a doctrinal consensus regarding Eucharist. While much progress has been made regarding our common doctrinal understanding of real presence, the official Catholic position asks for more than common belief in the real presence. Some Christians—Catholics included—hold that sharing Holy Communion is proper only between churches that have a historical succession of bishops and true priesthood. For real (valid) Eucharist, you need real priesthood. This is an important element of the Catholic position.

The official Catholic position holds that Holy Communion is not only a source of Christian unity but also a sign of unity—real unity, existing now. "Strengthened in holy Communion by the body of Christ, [the faithful] manifest in a concrete way the unity of the people of God that this sacrament aptly signifies and wondrously causes" (*Dogmatic Constitution on the Church*, 11).

We cannot put forth signs of unity when obvious division still exists. Receiving communion at the same altar is not a sign of unity when we do so with the intention of separating afterward to return to our various churches. In short, the Catholic Church teaches that we should not pretend to have true unity if, in reality, we are separated from other Christian bodies. These days, that separation is often seen as stemming not as much from a disagreement about basic beliefs as it is over mutual recognition of the validity of Holy Orders.

The Eucharist is more than food for the individual Christian. When we come together to celebrate the Eucharist we express who we are as Church. The liturgy, especially the Eucharist, "is the outstanding means whereby the faithful may express in their lives and manifest to others the mystery of Christ and the real nature of the true Church" (*Constitution on the Sacred Liturgy*, 2).

Church Law

Pope John Paul II explains the Catholic position regarding intercommunion in his encyclical letter on ecumenism, *That All May Be One*. He says that Vatican II's *Decree on Ecumenism*,

> pointing out that the post-Reformation communities lack the "fullness of unity with us which should flow from Baptism," observes that "especially because of the absence of the sacrament of Orders" they have not preserved the genuine and total reality of the Eucharistic mystery, even though "when they commemorate the Lord's death and resurrection in the Holy Supper, they profess that it signifies life in communion with Christ and they await his coming in glory." (67)

Consequently, the current law of the Church states that ordinarily Catholics can receive the sacraments only from Catholic ministers (*Code of Canon Law*, 844). The law itself, however, gives some exceptions to this general rule:

Whenever necessity requires it or true spiritual advantage suggests it, and provided that danger of error or indifferentism is avoided, the Christian faithful for whom it is physically or morally impossible to approach a Catholic minister are permitted to receive the sacraments of penance, Eucharist, and anointing of the sick from non-Catholic ministers in whose Churches these sacraments are valid. (Canon 844, 2)

Sharing Communion With Protestants

We have seen that the official Catholic position of restricting the sharing of Holy Communion is based on the principle that Eucharist is a sign of Church unity already actually achieved. But years ago the larger issues of Church unity and ministry did not play a determining role. Seminarians were once taught that Protestants could not receive Holy Communion at Mass because they did not believe in the real presence of Christ in the Eucharist. Different Protestant denominations vary in their understanding of Communion, though, and individuals may not fully comprehend or agree with what their church teaches. It is often dangerous to presume to know what someone else believes.

Although many Protestants have true belief in Christ's eucharistic presence, Church laws regarding their participation in Catholic Eucharist are more restrictive than those regarding the Orthodox Churches because we do not share with other

Christians the same degree of unity that we share with the Orthodox.

> If the danger of death is present or if, in the judgment of the diocesan bishop or conference of bishops, some other grave necessity urges it, Catholic ministers administer these same sacraments (penance, Eucharist, and anointing of the sick) licitly also to other Christians not having full communion with the Catholic Church, who cannot approach a minister of their own community and who seek such on their own accord, provided that they manifest Catholic faith in respect to these sacraments and are properly disposed. (Canon 844, 4)

The law allows for some exceptions—"when grave necessity urges it." The Application of Principles and Norms on Ecumenism (*Directory for Ecumenism,* 1993) lists examples of this "grave necessity."

Ordinarily, according to the *Directory for Ecumenism,* when a Catholic marries a Christian of another denomination, the Eucharist is not celebrated. The wedding liturgy is intended to be a sign of unity between the bride and groom, as well as the the unity of Christ and the Church. If one party and the non-Catholic guests cannot receive Holy Communion, the liturgy will make visible signs of division. Reception of Holy Communion by non-Catholics at a wedding can "only be exceptional" and under the following conditions: serious need (danger of death or other grave necessity); the inability to approach one's own minister; a voluntary request by the recipient; manifestation of Catholic faith in the sacrament; and proper disposition to receive the sacrament.

We have seen that the official Catholic position of restricting the sharing of Holy Communion is based on the principle that Eucharist is a sign of Church unity already actually achieved. But years ago the larger issues of Church unity and ministry did not play a determining role. In the not too distant past, it was taught that Protestants could not receive Holy Communion at Mass because they did not believe in the real presence of Christ in the Eucharist. It was never explained exactly what they did believe, but it was not what we believed.

First Communion

Normally, adults who convert to the Catholic faith prepare for full initiation into the Church through a formation process called RCIA (the Rite of Christian Initiation of Adults). The high point of that process takes place at Easter Vigil, when the one who has been preparing (the catechumen) receives baptism, confirmation, and First Holy Communion (the sacraments of initiation) during the Church's solemn celebration of Christ's resurrection. Children, on the other hand, are usually welcomed to First Communion at the age of seven (the supposed age of reason) after a period of preparation.

Author Carol Luebering sees First Communion for children as an invitation to join the family table. She identifies a toddler's move from high chair to the family table as a momentous event, noting that a high chair is a throne for a small despot whose demands for another bite take precedence over others' needs. Its tray catches dribbled milk and mushy graham crackers; it provides a safety net for the messy process of learning to use a spoon.

A seat at the table acclaims a new status: The child is now a big boy or big girl. The move to the table brings new privileges. There a child can share fully in the family fare (even the broccoli!) and in the table conversation. The move also brings new responsibilities. The little one must master the rudiments of table manners. Children who sit at the table are expected to contribute something to the well-being of the whole family.

First Communion is just such a momentous move. A child, baptized as an infant into the family of God we call Church, at last takes a place at the Lord's table with the grownups. Grandparents, aunts, and friends join the youngster's immediate family in celebrating the event. The move also has meaning for the rest of us. We smile at the tykes in their First Communion finery—not just because they look cute but because they are joining us at our family table, too—the table of God's family.

All living creatures eat, but only human beings share a meal. A pride of lions dine on the same carcass, but the king gets his share first. Lionesses and cubs must wait their turn to snarl at each other over the leftovers, and the weakest ones eat last. Only in the human family is food truly shared. A family meal affirms the sharing of resources, the mutual love and interdependence that is the very essence of family. It is the daily rediscovery and celebration of what it means to be family.

Also uniquely human is the ability to add meaning to a special meal. A birthday dinner, a holiday feast, a picnic outing—very young children know that these are not everyday meals. They are set apart from the ordinary by different foods, seasonal decorations or unusual surroundings, the best china or colorful paper plates, perhaps by special songs and rituals (Christmas carols, carving the bird, blowing out the birthday candles). And they often include guests: extended family, neighbors, friends, coworkers.

Such special meals celebrate who we are. They emphasize our connections with one another even beyond the boundaries of immediate family. For countless generations, the Jews have annually celebrated the beginnings of their national identity—their flight from Egypt and their adoption as God's people—with a feast at the family table: the seder or Passover meal. It remains a family meal, celebrated at home.

Jesus celebrated the Passover meal as he grew up in Nazareth. On the night before he died, he celebrated it with his adopted family, his closest followers. Departing from the familiar ritual, he broke the unleavened bread for them and passed a cup of wine, declaring this food to be his body and blood, given for the life of the world. In this action, he gave us the Eucharist, the family meal that unites believers all around the world at one table. Accordingly, the first Christians, still rooted in Judaism, went to synagogues to pray and hear God's word, but they celebrated Eucharist in homes with those who had become family through Jesus.

Family traditions change, even though slowly. As the Church grew, the sacraments of initiation became separate moments. Confirmation and Communion were gradually postponed until children, like adult catechumens, were schooled in the faith by lesson and by example. By the tenth century, the three sacraments of initiation had become separated. First communicants were usually twelve to fourteen years old—nearly adults—until 1910, when Pope Pius X lowered the age for first reception to six or seven, or "the age of reason."

Vestiges of earlier traditions still cling to the celebration of First Communion today. Special occasions require special clothing, and in most parishes first communicants dress up for the occasion. Wise parents, however, keep the emphasis on the occasion and not the clothing! These children also dressed up for baptism, putting on the white garment that represented the risen Christ living in them, as newly baptized adults do today. Whether the baby wears an heirloom christening dress or simple white cloth, the fundamental meaning of the baptismal garment is the same.

In some parishes, First Communion is held apart from a regular weekend liturgy, in a special Mass where the children in a First Communion class or classes receives the sacrament as a group. In other parishes, children receive their First Communion individually, with their families at a regular weekend liturgy.

At the Passover meal, the smallest child at the table has an important role to play. It is their job to ask, "Why is this night different from all others?" Once this question is posed, the adults present retell the story of how God freed their ancestors and made them God's own people.

No first communicant needs to ask that question at Mass. The Eucharistic Prayer retells for all who are gathered there the story of Jesus' Passover from death to life, of our escape from sin and death and our adoption as God's sons and daughters. We repeat it because Christians of all ages need to remember it—not just once a year, not even once a week, but every day of our lives. Jesus' story is our story. His victory over sin and death makes us who we are.

Much of a child's learning occurs at mealtime, beginning with the cuddling that makes warm milk from breast or bottle taste sweeter. It grows by leaps and bounds when the child takes a seat at the family table. Sharing the day's happenings gives a little one a keener sense of what is important to this family. Older members add family history—memories of that unimaginable time when

Mommy was a little girl, stories of how grandparents met, fond anecdotes about present and past family members.

The same is true of God's table. There all God's children not only repeat Jesus' story; they also express in their conversations with God and with one another what is important to this Church family, this parish family.

All along, a first communicant has been learning the meaning of Christian identity from others—saying prayers with parents and helping to set up the Christmas crèche. Very young children catch a high-chair glimpse of the parish family at prayer, and gain an impression of the eucharistic meal. The shushing finger on a parent's lips conveys that something important is happening here; people's reverence at Communion tells the child that what is dispensed from those shiny dishes is special indeed.

Questions for Reflection

1. How would you explain the phrase "real presence" to someone who thinks the bread and wine at Mass merely symbolize Jesus' presence?

2. In what ways do you see Communion as a sign and symbol of unity?

3. What are your memories of receiving First Communion? If you are not a Catholic, what does Communion mean to you?

Conclusion

The Greek word *eucharistia* is generally translated as "thanksgiving." St. Paul used that term in his account of the Last Supper: "The Lord Jesus on the night he was betrayed, took bread and, giving thanks (*euchaistesas*), broke it and said, 'Take, eat, this is my body'" (see 1 Corinthians 11:23–24). Soon the whole celebration was called "the thanksgiving."

When we look at the etymology of *eucharistia* we see it comes from joining two Greek words: *eu*, meaning "good," and *charis*, "gift." Literally, then, both the sacrament of Eucharist and the celebration of it are "the good gifts" given to us as a legacy and memorial by Jesus Christ our Lord.

For all we have said here about the Eucharist, it remains an inexhaustible mystery. The Second Vatican Council labeled it the "source and summit of the Christian life." Reception of Jesus Christ in Holy Communion and adoration of him in the Blessed Sacrament are gifts from God that promote and deepen our relationship with Jesus.

Sources

Some of the information in this book originally appeared in:

Doyle, Stephen, O.F.M. "Jesus Christ: Why the Word Become Flesh." *Catholic Update*, January 2001.

Feister, John. "The Real Presence: Jesus' Gift to the Church." *Catholic Update*, September 2001.

Luebering, Carol. "First Communion: Joining the Family Table." *Catholic Update,* April 1995.

McBride, Alfred, O.PRAEM. "Eucharist." *Catholic Update,* October 2006.

Mick, Lawrence E., "From Passover to Eucharist: God's Liberating Love." *Catholic Update,* March 2006.

———. "Finding Jesus in the Eucharist: Four Ways He Is Present." *Catholic Update,* July 2005.

Richstatter, Thomas, O.F.M. "Eucharist: Sign and Source of Christian Unity." *Catholic Update,* May 2000.

Rohr, Richard. "God's Love Is Free: The Banquet Says It All." *Catholic Update,* April 2002.

Shannon, William H. "Communion of Saints: Key to the Eucharist." *Catholic Update,* May 2005.

Contributors

Stephen Doyle, O.F.M., was a biblical scholar and theology professor who directed pilgrimages in Italy, Greece, and the Holy Land.

John Feister is editor-in-chief of *St. Anthony Messenger* magazine.

Norman Langenbrunner has written articles for *Liguorian*, *The Bible Today*, *St Anthony Messenger*, and *Catechist*.

Carol Luebering is the author of *Handing on the Faith: Your Child's First Communion*, and *Coping with Loss: Praying Your Way to Acceptance*.

Alfred McBride, O.PRAEM., is the author of *Staying Faithful Today: To God, Ourselves, One Another* and *The Story of the Church*.

Lawrence E. Mick is the author of *I Like Being in Parish Ministry: Presider* and hundreds of articles about liturgy.

Thomas Richstatter, O.F.M., is currently a faculty member at St. Meinrad School of Theology and author of *The Mass: A Guided Tour*.

Richard Rohr, O.F.M., is a popular speaker and prolific author on the spiritual life and the author of *Breathing Under Water: Spirituality and the Twelve Steps*.

William H. Shannon is professor emeritus of history at Nazareth College, Rochester, New York, and the author of *Thomas Merton: An Introduction*.